Portable BLENDER SMOOTHIE Recipe Book

BY
BRIONY
THOMPSON

Table of Content

INTRODUCTION

Smoothies make for quick, nutritious and delicious snacks or meals that can be enjoyed anywhere. But lugging a full-size blender around to whip up your favorite blends isn't very convenient, especially if you're always hopping from home to work to the gym. That's where the magic of portable blenders comes in!

Portable blenders provide all the power and versatility of blending but in a compact and travel-friendly size. Equipped with handy features like rechargeable batteries and BPA-free drinking jars, portable blenders let you easily craft smoothies, shakes, and more with no restrictions.

In this Portable Blender Smoothie Recipe Book, we've compiled over 100 tantalizing smoothie recipes that can be made anywhere with a portable blender. Divided into chapters focusing on tropical, berry, chocolate, fruit, special and health-conscious smoothie blends, you'll find nourishing recipes packed with fruits, veggies, protein and superfoods.

We'll also provide an overview of portable blenders, their key features and benefits, so you can learn how to maximize this convenient appliance. With the array of smoothie inspirations and handy blending tips in this book, you'll gain the skills and know-how to integrate portable blending into your on-the-go lifestyle.

So get ready to take your smoothies to go! Let's dive in and start blending.

OVERVIEW OF PORTABLE BLENDER

Whether you're constantly on the go or want the flexibility to blend up your favorite smoothie wherever you may be, a portable blender can be a handy kitchen appliance to have. Portable blenders provide an easy way to whip up quick blended drinks or meals without being confined to your kitchen. In this blog post, we'll explore what exactly portable blenders are, their key features, and the benefits they offer for an on-the-go lifestyle.

What is a Portable Blender?

A portable blender is a small, lightweight and compact blending device designed specifically for portability and use away from a standard kitchen setup. Portable blenders operate either using a rechargeable lithium battery or plug into a USB port for power. Their compact size takes up minimal space in your bag or car.

Features of Portable Blenders

- **Compact Size:** Designed to be easily portable and stored. Much smaller than conventional counter-top blenders.
- **Travel Bottles/Cups:** Comes with BPA-free bottles, cups, or jars that double as your blending container for direct drinking.
- **Rechargeable battery:** Allows you to blend without being restricted by access to a power outlet. Batteries can provide multiple uses per charge.
- **Lower Power:** Due to smaller motor sizes, portable blenders have lower wattages than full-sized blenders. Best for lighter blending tasks.
- **Easy to Clean:** Blending containers are detachable and dishwasher-safe for quick cleaning.

Benefits of Using a Portable Blender

- **Blend Anywhere** - Use at home, work, gym, or on the go. No power outlet required.
- **Portability** - Compact size takes up little space when traveling or commuting.
- **Convenience** - Quickly whip up smoothies, shakes, sauces, dips whenever you want.
- **Versatility** - Make everything from breakfast smoothies to cocktail mixes.
- **Healthy Habits** - Blend healthy drinks to take along to work, gym, or on errands.

A portable blender offers great convenience and versatility for an on-the-go lifestyle. Their compact size, rechargeable batteries, and ease of use let you blend up drinks or meals no matter where you are. Considering their affordability and usefulness, a portable blender can be a smart appliance investment for any busy household.

CHAPTERS

TROPICAL SMOOTHIES

01. MANGO COCONUT DELIGHT SMOOTHIE

Total Time: 5 Minutes | Serving: 1

Ingredients

- Coconut Water 1/2 cup of
- Mango Sorbet 1/2 cup of
- Ice 1/2 cup of

Instructions

1. Add 1/2 cup of coconut water.
2. Add 1/2 cup of mango sorbet.
3. Screw on the lid to your BlendJet portable blender and blend.
4. Add 1/2 cup of crushed ice.
5. Screw on the lid to your BlendJet portable blender and blend your homemade mango smoothie until smooth!
6. Voila! You have the Mango Coconut Delight smoothie. Hydrate and enjoy!

02. MANGO BANANA SMOOTHIE

Total Time: 5 Minutes | Serving: 1

Ingredients

- 1 cup of Milk of Choice
- 1/2 Frozen Banana
- 1/4 cup of Yogurt of Choice
- 1 cup of Frozen Mango

Instructions

1. Add all ingredients ti your BlendJet
2. Blend for 1-2 cycles
3. Enjoy!

03. AÇAÍ SMOOTHIE

Total Time: 5 Minutes | Serving: 1

Ingredients

- 100g Açaí
- 1/2 cup of Milk of Choice
- 1 Frozen Banana
- 1 tbsp Agave

Instructions

1. Add all ingredients to the portable blender, and blend for 1-2 cycles.
2. Pour into a bowl, and top with your favorite toppings! We love adding fruits and seeds. Enjoy!

04. MANGO JACKFRUIT SMOOTHIE

Total Time: 5 Minutes | Serving: 1

Ingredients

- 1/2 cup of Frozen Pitaya Foods Jackfruit Pieces
- 1 tbsp Agave
- 1/2 Frozen Banana
- 1/4 cup of Coconut Water
- 1/4 cup of Frozen Mango

Instructions

1. Add all ingredients to your BlendJet
2. Blend for 2-3 cycles, or until smooth
3. Enjoy!

05. PAPAYA SMOOTHIE

Total Time: 5 Minutes | Serving: 1

Ingredients

- 1/4 cup of Papaya
- 2 tsp Vanilla Extract
- 1/4 cup of Yogurt of Choice
- 1 Banana
- Ice Cubes (as needed, float to top)
- 1/2 cup of Milk of Choice

Instructions

1. Add all ingredients to your BlendJet
2. Blend for 1 cycle
3. Sip and enjoy!

06. STRAWBERRY WATERMELON SMOOTHIE

Total Time: 5 Minutes | Serving: 1

Ingredients

- 1 cup of Frozen Strawberries
- A few Ice Cubes
- 1 cup of Watermelon Chunks
- 1/2 Lime
- Juice of 1 Lime

Instructions

1. Add all ingredients to your BlendJet XL Jar
2. Blend for 1-2 cycles
3. Enjoy!

07. AVOCADO KIWI SMOOTHIE

Total Time: 5 Minutes | Serving: 1

Ingredients

- 1/2 Haas Avocado, Peeled and Diced
- Ice Cubes (as needed, float to the top)
- 1 cup of Milk of Choice
- 1/2 cup of Yogurt of Choice
- 1 Kiwi
- 1 tbsp Honey

Instructions

1. Add all your ingredients into your portable Blender.
2. Blend for 1-2 cycles
3. Sip and enjoy!

08. KIWI SMOOTHIE

Total Time: 5 Minutes | Serving: 1

Ingredients

- 1/2 cup of Frozen Pineapple
- 1 cup of Milk of Choice
- 1/2 Frozen Banana
- 1 Kiwi
- Small handful of Spinach

Instructions

1. Add all ingredients to your BlendJet
2. Blend for 1-2 cycles
3. Garnish with a kiwi slice and enjoy!

BERRY SMOOTHIES

09. BERRY BREAKFAST SMOOTHIE

Total Time: 5 Minutes | Serving: 1

Ingredients

- 2 tbsp Uncooked Oatmeal
- 1/3 cup of Almond Milk
- 3 Frozen Strawberries
- 1 Frozen Banana

Instructions

1. Add 1/3 cup of almond milk to your BlendJet.
2. Add 2 tbsp uncooked oatmeal.
3. Screw on the lid to your BlendJet portable blender and blend until smooth.
4. Remove your BlendJet lid and add 3 frozen strawberries.
5. Screw on your lid back on, flip your BlendJet upside down and turn it on.
6. Flip your BlendJet right-side up and blend until smooth.

10. RASPBERRY GRAPEFRUIT SMOOTHIE

Total Time: 5 Minutes | Serving: 1

Ingredients

- 1 cup of Frozen Raspberries
- 1 cup of Pink Grapefruit Juice
- 1 tbsp Agave
- 1/2 Frozen Banana

Instructions

1. Add all ingredients to your BlendJet
2. Blend for 1-2 cycles
3. Enjoy!

11. BERRY BLUE SMOOTHIE

Total Time: 5 Minutes | Serving: 1

Ingredients

- 1/2 cup of Almond Milk
- 1/2 cup of Strawberries
- 1/2 cup of Blueberries

Instructions

1. Add 1/2 cup of almond milk.
2. Add 1/2 cup of strawberries.
3. Add 1/2 cup of blueberries.
4. Screw on the lid to your BlendJet portable blender and blend until smooth!

12. STRAWBERRY CHEESECAKE SMOOTHIE

Total Time: 5 Minutes | Serving: 1

Ingredients

- 1 tbsp Cream Cheese
- 1 tbsp Agave
- 1 cup of Milk of Choice
- 1/2 cup of Yogurt of Choice
- 1 tsp Vanilla Extract
- 1 cup of Strawberries

Instructions

1. Add all ingredients into your portable blender
2. Blend for 1 cycle
3. Top with whipped cream, graham cracker crumbs and strawberry to garnish
4. Sip and enjoy!

13. STRAWBERRY SMOOTHIE

Total Time: 5 Minutes | Serving: 1

Ingredients

- ½ banana peeled
- ½ cup of passion fruit juice
- ¾ cup of frozen strawberries

Instructions

1. Place the banana, frozen strawberries, and passion fruit juice into your BlendJet – in that order.
2. Double-press the power button to enter pulse mode. The blue light will flash 3 times and the swirl will stay lit up while pulse mode is on.
3. Press the button a few times to pulse the mixture a few times. Pulse until smooth.
4. Pour into a glass and enjoy immediately!

14. HONEY FIG SMOOTHIE

Total Time: 5 Minutes | Serving: 1

Ingredients

- 1 tbsp Honey
- 4 Figs, Halved
- 1/4 cup of Yogurt of Choice
- 1/2 Frozen Banana
- 1/2 cup of Milk of Choice

Instructions

1. Blend all ingredients in your BlendJet for 1-2 cycles and enjoy!

15. RASPBERRY SMOOTHIE

Total Time: 5 Minutes | Serving: 1

Ingredients

- 4 fl ounce Frozen Raspberries
- 2 tsp Honey
- 2 tbsp Unsweetened Almond Milk
- 5 Ice Cubes
- 4 tbsp Plain Greek Yogurt
- 4 fl ounce Apple Juice

Instructions

1. Add frozen raspberries and ingredients to BlendJet 2
2. Blend until smooth
3. Drink straight from the BlendJet 2

16. CHERRY SMOOTHIE

Total Time: 5 Minutes | Serving: 1

Ingredients

- 1 cup of Milk of Choice
- 1 cup of Cherries
- 1/2 Frozen Banana
- 1/2 tsp Vanilla Extract
- 1 tbsp Almond Butter
- 1/4 cup of Yogurt of Choice

Instructions

1. Add all ingredients to your BlendJet
2. Blend for 1-2 cycles
3. Enjoy!

17. BLUEBERRY COCONUT SMOOTHIE

Total Time: 5 Minutes | Serving: 1

Ingredients

- Ice Cubes (float to the top)
- 1/2 Frozen Banana
- 1 cup of Coconut Milk
- 1 cup of Frozen Blueberries
- 1 tbsp Cacao Powder

Instructions

1. Add all ingredients to your BlendJet
2. Blend for 1-2 cycles
3. Drink straight from the BlendJet and enjoy!

18. BLACKBERRY SMOOTHIE

Total Time: 5 Minutes | Serving: 1

Ingredients

- 1/2 Frozen Banana
- 1 Lemon
- 1/4 cup of Yogurt of Choice
- 1 cup of Milk of Choice
- 1 cup of Frozen Blackberries

Instructions

1. Add all ingredients to your BlendJet
2. Blend for 1-2 cycles
3. Enjoy!

19. LEMON RASPBERRY SMOOTHIE

Total Time: 5 Minutes | Serving: 1

Ingredients

- 1 cup of Frozen Raspberries
- 1 tbsp Lemon Juice
- 1 cup of Milk of Choice
- 1/4 cup of Yogurt of Choice
- 1/2 Frozen Banana
- 1/2 tsp Lemon Zest

Instructions

1. Add all ingredients to your BlendJet
2. Blend for 1-2 cycles
3. Sip and enjoy!

20. BLACKBERRY COBBLER SMOOTHIE

Total Time: 5 Minutes | Serving: 1

Ingredients

- 1 cup of Milk of Choice
- 1 cup of Frozen Blackberries
- 1/4 cup of Yogurt of Choice
- Ice Cubes (float to the top)
- 1 tbsp Maple Syrup
- 2 tbsp Rolled Oats
- 1/4 tsp Cinnamon

Instructions

1. Add all ingredients to your BlendJet
2. Blend for 2-3 cycles
3. Top with frozen blackberries and enjoy!

21. BERRY COBBLER SMOOTHIE

Total Time: 5 Minutes | Serving: 1

Ingredients

- Ice Cubes (float to the top)
- 1 tbsp Maple Syrup
- 1/4 tsp Cinnamon
- 1/2 cup of Yogurt of Choice
- 1/4 tsp Vanilla
- 1/2 cup of Oats
- 1 cup of Milk of Choice
- 1 cup of Frozen Mixed Berries

Instructions

1. Add all your ingredients into your BlendJet
2. Blend for 1-2 cycles
3. Top with whipped cream of choice, fresh berries and enjoy!

22. BERRY COLLAGEN PEPTIDES SMOOTHIE

Total Time: 5 Minutes | Serving: 1

Ingredients

- 1 tbsp Chia Seeds
- 1/2 Banana
- 1/2 cup of Frozen Mixed Berries
- 1 scoop Vital Proteins Collagen Peptides
- 1 tbsp Nut Butter of Choice
- 3/4 cup of Milk of Choice
- Ice Cubes (float to the top)

Instructions

1. Add all ingredients into your portable blender
2. Blend for 1-2 cycles
3. Pour into a glass or drink right from your BlendJet and enjoy!

23. RASPBERRY LIME SMOOTHIE

Total Time: 5 Minutes | Serving: 1

Ingredients

- 1 cup of Yogurt of Choice
- 1 cup of Milk of Choice
- 1 cup of Frozen Raspberries
- 1 tbsp Agave
- Juice of 1 Lime
- Zest of 1 Lime

Instructions

1. Add all your ingredients into your BlendJet
2. Blend for 1-2 cycles
3. Top with a lime and enjoy!

24. MIXED BERRY SMOOTHIE

Total Time: 5 Minutes | Serving: 1

Ingredients

- 1/2 Frozen Banana
- 1 tbsp Maple Syrup
- 1 cup of Milk of Choice
- 1 cup of Frozen Mixed Berries

Instructions

1. Add all your ingredients into your BlendJet
2. Blend for 2 cycles
3. Sip and enjoy!

25. CRANBERRY APPLE SMOOTHIE

Total Time: 5 Minutes | Serving: 1

Ingredients

- 1/4 tsp Cinnamon
- 1 cup of Milk of Choice
- 1/2 Banana
- 1-2 tbsp Maple Syrup
- 1/3 cup of Cranberry
- 1/2 Apple, Peeled, Cored, Diced

Instructions

1. Add all your ingredients into your BlendJet
2. Blend for 2 cycles
3. Sip and enjoy!

26. BERRY AND BEET SMOOTHIE

Total Time: 5 Minutes | Serving: 1

Ingredients

- 1/4 cup of Chopped Beets
- 1 cup of Frozen Mixed Berries
- 1 cup of Milk of Choice
- 1 tbsp Agave
- 1 tbsp Lemon Juice

Instructions

1. Add all your ingredients into your BlendJet
2. Blend for 1-2 cycles
3. Sip and enjoy!

27. COCONUT GOJI BERRY SMOOTHIE

Total Time: 5 Minutes | Serving: 1

Ingredients

- 1 cup of Coconut Milk
- 1/2 Frozen Banana
- 3 tbsp Goji Berries
- 1 cup of Frozen Mixed Berries
- Ice Cubes (float to the top)
- 1 tsp Chia Seeds

Instructions

1. Add all ingredients to your BlendJet
2. Blend for 2-3 cycles
3. Sip and enjoy!

CHOCOLATE & NUT SMOOTHIES

28. CHOCOLATE SMOOTHIE

Total Time: 5 Minutes | Serving: 1

Ingredients

- 1/4 cup of your choice of cocoa
- 1/2 cup of pitted dates
- 1/2 cup of silken tofu
- 3 ice cubes
- 3 Tbsp boiling water
- 1/4 cup of almonds

Instructions

1. Add the dates, almonds, and your choice of cocoa or chocolate syrup to your Fresh Juicer Portable Blender.
2. Pour the boiling water over the ingredients and allow it to sit for about 10 minutes. This step is key to softening the ingredients and releasing their delectable flavors.
3. After 10 minutes, add in the silken tofu and ice cubes.
4. Secure the lid and blend for about 30 seconds, or until you achieve your desired smoothie consistency. With the Fresh Juicer Portable Blender, it's all about your personal preference.

29. CHOCOLATE PEANUT BUTTER SMOOTHIE

Total Time: 5 Minutes | Serving: 1

Ingredients

- 1 banana
- 1 cup of mlk Of Choice
- 1/4 cup of eanut Butter
- 1 tbsp aple Syrup
- 1/4 cup of ocoa Powder

Instructions

1. Add all your ingredients into your BlendJet
2. Blend for 1 cycle
3. Sip and enjoy!

30. FROSTED SUGAR COOKIE SMOOTHIE

Total Time: 5 Minutes | Serving: 1

Ingredients

- 2 tbsp Vanilla Frosting Of Choice
- 1/4 cup of Yogurt Of Choice
- 1 Cup of Milk Of Choice
- Ice Cubes float to top with
- 1/8 tsp Almond Extract

Instructions

1. Add all ingredients to your BlendJet
2. Blend for 1-2 cycles
3. Rim the BlendJet with sprinkles
4. Top with whipped cream of choice and more sprinkles
5. Sip and enjoy!

31. CHOCOLATE CHERRY SMOOTHIE

Total Time: 5 Minutes | Serving: 1

Ingredients

- 1/2 Frozen Banana
- 1 cup of Cherries
- 1 cup of Chocolate Milk

Instructions

1. Put everything in your BlendJet and blend it for one to two cycles. Then, enjoy!

32. CARAMEL MOCHA SMOOTHIE

Total Time: 5 Minutes | Serving: 1

Ingredients

- 2 tbsp Cocoa Powder
- 1 cup of Milk of Choice
- 1 tbsp Caramel
- 1/2 tsp Vanilla Extract
- 1 tbsp Maple Syrup
- 1/4 cup of Chilled Coffee
- Ice Cubes (to float on top)

Instructions

1. Put everything into your BlendJet and set it to full speed for one cycle.
2. Sprinkle your favorite whipped cream and caramel on top.
3. Drink and have fun!

33. CHOCOLATE CHIP COOKIE DOUGH SMOOTHIE

Total Time: 5 Minutes | Serving: 1

Ingredients

- 1 cup of Milk of Choice
- 1 pack TUSOL Cacao + Lion's Mane Smoothie Pack
- 1/4 cup of Chocolate Chips
- 1 tbsp Maple Syrup
- 3/4 tsp Vanilla Extract
- Pinch of Salt
- 1 tbsp Peanut Butter

Instructions

1. Use the BlendJet to blend everything for three to four cycles, and then enjoy!

34. CHESTNUT OAT SMOOTHIE

Total Time: 5 Minutes | Serving: 1

Ingredients

- 1/4 tsp Cinnamon
- 1/4 cup of Cooked and Peeled Chestnuts
- 1/4 cup of Yogurt of Choice
- 1/2 tsp Vanilla Extract
- 1/8 tsp Nutmeg
- 1 cup of Oat Milk
- Ice Cubes (to float on top)

Instructions

1. Blend all of the ingredients in your BlendJet for one to two cycles, and then enjoy!

35. PECAN PIE SMOOTHIE

Total Time: 5 Minutes | Serving: 1

Ingredients

- 1 tbsp Maple Syrup
- 1 tsp Vanilla Extract
- 1 cup of Milk of Choice
- Dash of Cinnamon
- Pinch of Salt
- 1/4 cup of Cashews
- 1/3 cup of Pecans
- 1/2 cup of Coconut Jelly
- 1/2 Frozen Banana

Instructions

1. Use your BlendJet to mix everything, and then have fun!

36. MUD PIE SMOOTHIE

Total Time: 5 Minutes | Serving: 1

Ingredients

- 1 Frozen Banana
- 1/4 cup of Chocolate Sauce
- 2 cups of Milk of Choice
- 1/4 cup of Crushed Oreos
- 1/2 tsp Vanilla Extract

Instructions

1. Putting everything into your BlendJet and setting it to two cycles
2. Pour into glasses and top with whipped cream of your choice.
3. Put chocolate sauce on top and serve!

37. CHOCOLATE AVOCADO SMOOTHIE

Total Time: 5 Minutes | Serving: 1

Ingredients

- 1/2 Banana
- 1 cup of Milk of Choice
- 1/2 tsp Vanilla Extract
- 1/2 Avocado
- 2 tbsp Maple Syrup
- 3 tbsp Cocoa Powder
- Ice Cubes (to float on top)

Instructions

1. Put everything into your BlendJet and blend for one to two cycles.
2. You can drink straight from your BlendJet and enjoy it!

38. CHOCOLATE COLLAGEN SMOOTHIE

Total Time: 5 Minutes | Serving: 1

Ingredients

- 1 Banana
- 2 scoops Vital Proteins Chocolate Collagen Powder
- 2 ounce Iced Coffee
- 1/2 cup of Milk of Choice
- Ice Cubes (to float on top)
- Chocolate Chips (for topping)

Instructions

1. Put everything into the BlendJet and blend for one to two cycles.
2. Put Greek yogurt on top, take a sip, and enjoy!

39. PEANUT BUTTER CUP OF SMOOTHIE

Total Time: 5 Minutes | Serving: 1

Ingredients

- 1 cup of Milk of Choice
- 2 tbsp Peanut Butter
- 1/2 Frozen Banana
- 2 tbsp Cocoa Powder
- Ice Cubes (to float on top)

Instructions

1. Put everything into your BlendJet and blend for one to two cycles.
2. Add peanut butter cup of pieces on top, and enjoy!

40. PEANUT BUTTER OATMEAL SMOOTHIE

Total Time: 5 Minutes | Serving: 1

Ingredients

- 1 tsp ground cinnamon
- 1 cup of oat milk (or any milk)
- ⅛ tsp salt
- ½ cup of rolled oats or quick oats
- 2 tbsp peanut butter
- 2 frozen ripe bananas, peeled before freezing
- 1 tsp vanilla extract
- 1 tbsp ground flaxseed (optional)
- 1–2 tbsp maple syrup (optional but recommended)

Instructions

1. Put everything into your Fresh Juice portable Blender.
2. Blend the ingredients between 2 and 3 cycles until they are smooth and creamy.
3. Pour it into a glass and top it with peanut butter. You can drink it straight from the bottle.
4. Have fun!

41. PECAN SMOOTHIE

Total Time: 5 Minutes | Serving: 1

Ingredients

- 1/2 cup of Yogurt of Choice
- 1/2 tsp Vanilla Extract
- 1/2 tsp Cinnamon
- 1/2 tsp Melted Butter of Choice
- 1 tbsp Maple Syrup
- 2 tbsp Pecans
- 1 cup of Milk of Choice
- Ice Cubes (to float on top)

Instructions

1. Put everything into your BlendJet and blend for one to two cycles.
2. Add your favorite whipped cream and chopped pecans on top.
3. Drink and have fun!

42. MANGO SMOOTHIE

Total Time: 5 Minutes | Serving: 1

Ingredients

- 1/2 Frozen Banana
- 1 cup of Milk of Choice
- 1 cup of Frozen Mango
- Ice Cubes (to float on top)

Instructions

1. Put everything into your BlendJet and blend for one to two cycles.
2. Drink and have fun!

43. APPLE OATS SMOOTHIE

Total Time: 5 Minutes | Serving: 1

Ingredients

- 1/4 cup of Oats
- 3/4 cup of Milk of Choice
- 1/8 tsp Cinnamon
- 1 Apple, Chopped Into Pieces
- 1 tbsp Honey
- 2 Medjool Dates, Pitted
- Ice Cubes (to float on top)

Instructions

1. Mix everything until it's smooth, and then enjoy!

44. PEANUT BUTTER BANANA SMOOTHIE

Total Time: 5 Minutes | Serving: 1

Ingredients

- 1 cup of Milk of Choice
- 1/4 cup of Oats
- 1/4 tsp Vanilla
- 1 tbsp Maple Syrup
- 1/4 cup of Peanut Butter
- 1 Banana

Instructions

1. Put everything into the BlendJet and set it to 2 to 4 cycles.
2. Drink and have fun!

45. BLUEBERRY BANANA SMOOTHIE

Total Time: 5 Minutes | Serving: 1

Ingredients

- 1/2 cup of Unsweetened Vanilla Almond Milk
- A drizzle of Maple Syrup
- 1/4 cup of Blueberries
- 1/2 Frozen Banana
- A dash of Turmeric

Instructions

1. Put 1/2 cup of unsweetened vanilla almond milk into your BlendJet.
2. Cut up half of a frozen banana into thin slices.
3. Put in 1/4 cup of blueberries.
4. Put a little maple syrup and turmeric on top.
5. Put your BlendJet's lid back on and blend until smooth.
6. Use the BlendJet portable blender to make this easy blueberry banana smoothie. Sip and enjoy!

46. PEACH SMOOTHIE

Total Time: 5 Minutes | Serving: 1

Ingredients

- Milk Of Choice
- 1/4 Banana
- 3/4 cup of Milk of Choice
- 1/2 cup of Frozen Peaches
- 1/4 tsp Vanilla

Instructions

1. Put everything into the BlendJet and let it run for one cycle.
2. Have fun!

47. RASPBERRY WHITE CHOCOLATE SMOOTHIE

Total Time: 5 Minutes | Serving: 1

Ingredients

- 1 cup of Milk of Choice
- 3/4 cup of Frozen Raspberries
- 1/2 cup of Yogurt of Choice
- 2 tbsp White Chocolate Chips

Instructions

1. Combine all the ingredients in your BlendJet and blend for two to three cycles.
2. Add your favorite whipped cream on top, and enjoy!

48. POMEGRANATE SMOOTHIE

Total Time: 5 Minutes | Serving: 1

Ingredients

- 1 tbsp Agave (or sweetener of choice
- 1 cup of Oatly Milk (or milk of choice)
- 1/2 cup of Pomegranate Arils
- 1/2 Frozen Banana

Instructions

1. Put everything into your BlendJet and blend for one to two cycles.
2. Have fun!

49. BANANA BREAD SMOOTHIE

Total Time: 5 Minutes | Serving: 2

Ingredients

- 1 Frozen Banana
- Pinch of Nutmeg
- 1/4 tsp Cinnamon
- Pinch of Salt
- 2 cups of Milk of Choice
- 3/4 cup of Granola
- 1/2 tsp Vanilla Extract
- 1/2 cup of Yogurt of Choice

Instructions

1. Put everything into your BlendJet and blend for one to two cycles.
2. Put it in two glasses and enjoy!

50. APPLE CRUMBLE SMOOTHIE

Total Time: 5 Minutes | Serving: 1

Ingredients

- 1/4 tsp Cinnamon
- 2 tbsp Rolled Oats
- 1/4 cup of Yogurt of Choice
- 1 cup of Milk of Choice
- 1/2 cup of Peeled Apples
- 1 tbsp Maple Syrup
- Ice Cubes (to float on top)

Instructions

1. Put everything into your BlendJet and set it to two or three cycles.
2. Put some granola on top, and enjoy!

51. MANGO PINEAPPLE GREEN TEA SMOOTHIE

Total Time: 5 Minutes | Serving: 1

Ingredients

- 1/2 Frozen Banana
- 1/2 cup of Frozen Pineapple
- 1/2 cup of Frozen Mango
- 1 tbsp Agave (or sweetener of choice)
- 1 cup of Green Tea (cooled)
- Ice Cubes (to float on top)

Instructions

1. Put everything into your BlendJet and blend for one to two cycles.
2. Add a slice of pineapple on top and enjoy!

52. BLUEBERRY CHEESECAKE SMOOTHIE

Total Time: 5 Minutes | Serving: 1

Ingredients

- 1 cup of Milk of Choice
- 1 tbsp Cream Cheese
- 1/4 tsp Vanilla Extract
- 1 cup of Frozen Blueberries
- 1 tbsp Agave (or sweetener of choice)
- 1/2 cup of Yogurt of Choice
- Ice Cubes (to float on top)

Instructions

1. Put everything into your BlendJet and blend for one to two cycles.
2. Add your favorite whipped cream, graham cracker crumbs, and fresh blueberries on top, and then enjoy!

53. CUCUMBER APPLE MINT SMOOTHIE

Total Time: 5 Minutes | Serving: 1

Ingredients

- Water
- 1 cup of Cucumber, sliced
- 1/2 cup of Apple Juice
- 1/2 cup of Water
- 1/4 cup of Mint, chopped
- Ice Cubes (to float on top

Instructions

1. Put everything into your BlendJet and blend for three to four cycles.
2. Drink and have fun!

54. KALE COCONUT SMOOTHIE

Total Time: 5 Minutes | Serving: 1

Ingredients

- 1/2 Kiwi
- 1/2 cup of Coconut Milk
- 1/2 Frozen Banana
- 1 cup of Kale
- 1/2 cup of Water
- 1 tbsp Coconut Flakes
- Ice Cubes (to float on top)

Instructions

1. Put everything into your BlendJet and set it to 2 to 4 cycles.
2. Drink and have fun!

55. LEMON PINEAPPLE SMOOTHIE

Total Time: 5 Minutes | Serving: 1

Ingredients

- 1/4 cup of Lemon Juice
- 1/2 Frozen Banana
- 3/4 cup of Milk of Choice
- 1/2 cup of Frozen Pineapple
- 1/4 cup of Yogurt of Choice
- Ice Cubes (to float on top)

Instructions

1. Put everything into your BlendJet and set it to two cycles.
2. Drink and have fun!

56. APPLE CARROT ORANGE SMOOTHIE

Total Time: 5 Minutes | Serving: 1

Ingredients

- 1 tbsp Maple Syrup
- 1/2 cup of Carrots
- 1/2 cup of Peeled Oranges
- 1 cup of Milk of Choice
- 1/2 cup of Peeled Apples

Instructions

1. Put everything into your BlendJet and set it to two or three cycles.
2. Drink and have fun!

57. CITRUS SMOOTHIE

Total Time: 5 Minutes | Serving: 1

Ingredients

- 1/8 tsp Turmeric
- 1/8 tsp Ginger
- 1/2 Lemon Juice
- 1 cup of Orange Juice
- 1/4 cup of Frozen Mango
- 1/4 cup of Coconut Yogurt
- 1/2 Frozen Banana
- 1/4 cup of Carrots
- 1/4 tsp Cinnamon

Instructions

1. Put everything into the BlendJet and blend for two to four cycles.

58. PITAYA SMOOTHIE

Total Time: 5 Minutes | Serving: 1

Ingredients

- 1 cup of Pitaya Frozen Dragon Fruit Cubes
- 1/2 cup of Mango
- 6 ounce Apple Juice
- 1 Banana

Instructions

1. Put everything into the BlendJet and blend for one to two cycles.

59. WATERMELON SMOOTHIE

Total Time: 10 Minutes | Serving: 1

Ingredients

- 2 ounce Almond Milk or Low-Fat Cow's Milk
- 1 small Lime Juice
- 1 sprig of Mint (approximately 4 inches)
- 12 ounce Frozen Watermelon Cubes

Instructions

2. Charge BlendJet for an hour.
3. Line up the arrows on the base and jar.
4. Clean it with water and soap before using it for the first time.
5. Putting watermelon cubes in ziplock bags and freezing them will help when ready.
6. Pour the liquid and add the ingredients, leaving some room between them.
7. Keep the lid on for transport.
8. Press the "Power" button to blend. For regular, 20 seconds will do it; for thicker, repeat the process.

60. GRAPE SMOOTHIE

Total Time: 5 Minutes | Serving: 1

Ingredients

- 1/2 Frozen Banana
- 1 cup of Milk of Choice
- 1 cup of Frozen Red Grapes
- 1/4 cup of Yogurt of Choice

Instructions

1. Put everything into the BlendJet and blend for one to two cycles.
2. Have fun!

61. GRAPEFRUIT SMOOTHIE

Total Time: 5 Minutes | Serving: 1

Ingredients

- 1 cup of Apple Juice
- 1/2 Frozen Banana
- 2 tbsp Hemp Seeds
- 1 cup of Grapefruit Pieces, Peeled, No Seeds
- 1/4 cup of Yogurt of Choice

Instructions

1. Put everything into your BlendJet and blend for one to two cycles.
2. Put a grapefruit slice on top and enjoy!

62. APPLE PECAN SMOOTHIE

Total Time: 5 Minutes | Serving: 1

Ingredients

- 1 tbsp Maple Syrup
- 1 tsp Hemp Hearts
- 1/2 cup of Frozen Cranberries
- 1 cup of Milk of Choice
- 1 tbsp Pecans
- 1/2 cup of Apple, Chopped
- 1/4 tsp Cinnamon
- Ice Cubes (to float on top)

Instructions

1. Use the BlendJet to mix everything for one to two cycles, and then enjoy!

63. APPLE PIE SMOOTHIE

Total Time: 5 Minutes | Serving: 1

Ingredients

- 1 cup of Milk of Choice
- 1/2 tsp Vanilla Extract
- 1 tbsp Maple Syrup
- 1/2 Apple, Peeled, Cored, Diced
- 1/2 tsp Apple Pie Spice
- Ice Cubes (to float on top)

Instructions

1. Combine all of the ingredients in your BlendJet and blend for three cycles.
2. Spread your favorite whipped cream on top. Add an apple slice and cinnamon.
3. Drink and have fun!

64. S'MORES SMOOTHIE

Total Time: 5 Minutes | Serving: 1

Ingredients

- 1/2 Frozen Banana
- 2 tbsp Marshmallow Fluff
- 1 cup of Chocolate Milk
- 2 tbsp Graham Crackers
- 1 tbsp Maple Syrup
- Ice Cubes (to float on top)

Instructions

1. Put everything into your BlendJet.
2. Mix for one to two cycles.
3. Rim the BlendJet with Graham cracker crumbs.
4. Add chocolate syrup and mini marshmallows on top.
5. Drink and have fun!

65. STRAWBERRY SEA MOSS SMOOTHIE

Total Time: 5 Minutes | Serving: 1

Ingredients

- 1 cup of Milk of Choice
- 1 cup of Frozen Strawberries
- 1 tbsp Sea Moss
- 1/2 Frozen Banana

Instructions

1. Put everything into your BlendJet and blend for one to two cycles.
2. Add a strawberry on top and enjoy!

66. SPICED CHAI SMOOTHIE

Total Time: 5 Minutes | Serving: 1

Ingredients

- 1/4 tsp Ground Cardamom
- 1/4 tsp Ginger
- 1 scoop LyfeFuel Essentials (Vanilla Chai)
- A few Ice Cubes
- 1 cup of Chai Tea
- 1/2 Banana
- 1/2 cup of Milk of Choice
- 1/2 tsp Cinnamon

Instructions

1. Use your BlendJet to mix everything for one to two cycles, and then enjoy!

67. PUMPKIN SMOOTHIE

Total Time: 5 Minutes | Serving: 1

Ingredients

- 1/4 cup of Yogurt of Choice
- 1/2 tsp Cinnamon
- Pinch of Ginger
- 1 tsp Maple Syrup
- Pinch of Nutmeg
- 1/2 tsp Vanilla Extract
- 1 cup of Milk of Choice
- 1/2 Frozen Banana
- 1/2 cup of Pumpkin Puree

Instructions

1. Put everything into your BlendJet and blend for one to two cycles.
2. Add whipped cream and cinnamon on top, and then enjoy!

68. GRAPEFRUIT GINGER SMOOTHIE

Total Time: 5Minutes | Serving: 1

Ingredients

- 1/4 cup of Yogurt of Choice
- 1 tbsp Agave
- 1 tbsp Grated Ginger
- 1 cup of Grapefruit Juice
- 1/2 cup of Frozen Strawberries

Instructions

1. Put everything into your BlendJet and blend for one to two cycles.
2. Have fun!

69. BLACKBERRY LIME SMOOTHIE

Total Time: 5 Minutes | Serving: 1

Ingredients

- 1 cup of Milk of Choice
- 1 cup of Frozen Blackberries
- 1/2 Frozen Banana
- 1 tbsp Lime Juice
- 1/4 cup of Yogurt of Choice
- 1/2 tsp Lime Zest

Instructions

1. Put everything in your BlendJet and blend for one to two cycles.
2. Sip and enjoy!

70. UNICORN SMOOTHIE

Total Time: 5 Minutes | Serving: 1

Ingredients

- 1/2 Frozen Banana
- 1/4 cup of Frozen Dragon Fruit
- 1 tsp Dye-Free Sprinkles
- Coconut Whipped Cream (to your liking)

Instructions

1. Put everything into the BlendJet except the coconut whipped cream and sprinkles. Blend for one cycle.
2. Put it in a glass, then add coconut whipped cream and dye-free sprinkles on top!

71. BLUEBERRY CHIA SMOOTHIE

Total Time: 5 Minutes | Serving: 1

Ingredients

- 1 tbsp Maple Syrup
- 1/2 cup of Frozen Blueberries
- 1 tbsp Chia Seeds
- 1/4 tsp Vanilla Extract
- 1/2 Frozen Banana
- 1 cup of Milk of Choice
- 1/4 cup of Oats

Instructions

1. Put everything into the BlendJet and blend the blueberry chia smoothie for two to four cycles. Sip and enjoy!

72. CHERRY TART SMOOTHIE

Total Time: 5 Minutes | Serving: 1

Ingredients

- 1 cup of Milk of Choice
- 1 cup of Cherries
- 1/2 Frozen Banana
- 1/2 tsp Vanilla Extract
- 1/4 cup of Yogurt of Choice

Instructions

1. Put everything into your BlendJet and blend for one to two cycles.
2. Have fun!

73. VANILLA LATTE SMOOTHIE

Total Time: 5 Minutes | Serving: 1

Ingredients

- 1/2 tsp Vanilla Extract
- 1 tbsp Maple Syrup
- 1/2 cup of Milk of Choice
- 1/4 cup of Yogurt of Choice
- 1/2 cup of Chilled Coffee
- Ice Cubes (to float on top)

Instructions

1. Put everything into your BlendJet and set it to "Blend" for one cycle.
2. Add any whipped cream on top.
3. Drink and have fun!

74. PRESSED JUICERY SMOOTHIE

Total Time: 5 Minutes | Serving: 1

Ingredients

- 1/4 cup of Strawberries
- 1/2 Banana
- 6 ounce Pressed Juicery Chocolate Almond Milk
- Dash of Cinnamon
- 1 tbsp Peanut Butter
- 2 Ice Cubes

Instructions

1. Add Pressed Juicery Chocolate Almond Milk to your BlendJet to start making this chocolate strawberry smoothie.
2. Add the remaining ingredients to the BlendJet, blend for one cycle, and serve!

75. UNICORN SUPERFOODS SMOOTHIE

Total Time: 5 Minutes | Serving: 1

Ingredients

- 1 Frozen Banana
- 1 tsp Unicorn Superfoods Blue Spirulina
- 1/4 cup of Frozen Mango
- 1 cup of Plant-Based Milk

Instructions

1. Put everything into the BlendJet and blend for one cycle.
2. Sip and enjoy!

76. GINGERBREAD SMOOTHIE

Total Time: 5 Minutes | Serving: 1

Ingredients

- 1 tbsp Molasses
- 1 cup of Milk of Choice
- 1/2 tsp Vanilla Extract
- 1 tbsp Nut Butter of Choice
- 1/4 cup of Oats
- 1 tsp Gingerbread Spice
- Ice Cubes (to float on top)

Instructions

1. Put everything into the portable blender.
2. Using three cycles, blend.
3. Spread your favorite whipped cream on top. Add a gingerbread cookie and cinnamon.
4. Drink and have fun!

77. SPICED BANANA CHAI SMOOTHIE

Total Time: 5 Minutes | Serving: 1

Ingredients

- 3 tbsp Nut Butter
- 2 tsp Chai Spice
- 1 Frozen Banana
- 2 cups of Milk of Choice
- 1 tsp Vanilla Extract
- Ice Cubes (to float on top)

Instructions

1. Put everything in your BlendJet XL Jar and blend for one to two cycles.
2. Add banana slices, nut butter, and cinnamon on top of the mixture in two glasses.
3. Sip and have fun!

78. COFFEE SMOOTHIE

Total Time: 5 Minutes | Serving: 1

Ingredients

- 1/4 cup of Oatmeal
- 1/4 cup of Coffee
- 1/4 cup of Milk of Choice
- 1 Frozen Banana

Instructions

1. Add 1/4 cup of cold coffee, 1/4 cup of milk, 1/4 cup of oatmeal.
2. Put the BlendJet lid on top of the machine and blend!
3. Take off the blender's lid and add one frozen banana.
4. Put the lid back on your portable BlendJet blender and blend until smooth.

79. SUNSET SMOOTHIE

Total Time: 5 Minutes | Serving: 1

Ingredients

- 1/2 cup of Orange Juice
- 1 Banana
- Handful of Frozen Mango Chunks
- Handful of Pineapple Chunks

Instructions

1. Put in half a cup of your favorite orange juice.Cut up one banana and add it.
2. Put the lid back on your BlendJet and blend!
3. Add some chunks of pineapple.
4. Put the lid back on your BlendJet and blend!
5. Add some frozen mango chunks.
6. Put the lid back on your BlendJet and blend!

80. SWEET POTATO SMOOTHIE

Total Time: 5 Minutes | Serving: 1

Ingredients

- 1/4 tsp Cinnamon
- 1 cup of Milk of Choice
- 1/4 cup of Sweet Potato Purée
- 1/4 cup of Yogurt of Choice
- 1 tbsp Maple Syrup
- Ice Cubes (to float on top)

Instructions

1. Put everything into your BlendJet and blend for one to two cycles.
2. Put some cinnamon on top and enjoy!

81. LEMON MERINGUE SMOOTHIE

Total Time: 5 Minutes | Serving: 1

Ingredients

- 1/4 cup of Yogurt of Choice
- 1/4 cup of Lemon Juice
- 1 tbsp Marshmallow Fluff
- 1 cup of Milk of Choice
- 1/2 Lemon Zest
- Ice Cubes (to float on top)

Instructions

1. Put everything in your BlendJet and blend it for one to two cycles. Then, enjoy!

82. CARROT SMOOTHIE

Total Time: 5 Minutes | Serving: 1

Ingredients

- 1/2 Frozen Banana
- Pinch of Nutmeg
- 1 cup of Carrots
- 1 cup of Orange Juice
- 1/4 tsp Cinnamon
- 1/4 cup of Yogurt of Choice

Instructions

1. Blend all of the ingredients in your BlendJet for one to two cycles, and then enjoy!

83. CUCUMBER SMOOTHIE

Total Time: 5 Minutes | Serving: 1

Ingredients

- 1/4 cup of Yogurt of Choice
- 1 cup of Milk of Choice
- 1/2 cup of Cucumber Slices
- 1/2 cup of Frozen Pineapple
- 1/2 Frozen Banana
- Small Handful of Spinach

Instructions

1. Put everything into the BlendJet and blend for one to two cycles.
2. Have fun!

84. BEETROOT SMOOTHIE

Total Time: 5 Minutes | Serving: 1

Ingredients

- 1/2 cup of Frozen Raspberries
- 1/2 Frozen Banana
- 1/2 cup of Beets, peeled and chopped
- 1 cup of Orange Juice

Instructions

1. Use your BlendJet to mix everything, and then have fun!

85. BLOOD ORANGE BEET SMOOTHIE

Total Time: 5 Minutes | Serving: 1

Ingredients

- 1/2 cup of Milk of Choice
- 1 scoop Protein Powder
- 1/3 cup of Raw Beets, peeled and chopped
- 1 tbsp Almond Butter
- 2 tsp Cordyceps Mushroom Powder
- 1 Blood Orange, peeled and segmented
- 1/2 Frozen Banana

Instructions

1. Put everything into your BlendJet and enjoy!

86. PB&J SMOOTHIE

Total Time: 5 Minutes | Serving: 1

Ingredients

- 1/2 Frozen Banana
- 2 tbsp Peanut Butter
- 1 cup of Milk of Choice
- 1/2 cup of Frozen Raspberries
- 1/2 cup of Frozen Strawberries
- Pinch of Salt

Instructions

1. Put everything into your BlendJet and blend for one to two cycles.
2. Put peanut butter on top and serve!

87. TURMERIC CRUSH SMOOTHIE

Total Time: 5 Minutes | Serving: 1

Ingredients

- 1/2 cup of Frozen Pineapple
- 3/4 cup of Frozen Mango
- 1/2 Lemon Juice
- 1/2 cup of Orange Juice
- 1 tsp Turmeric
- 1 tsp Ginger, grated

Instructions

1. Put everything into your BlendJet and blend for one to two cycles.
2. Pour some beet and carrot juice into a glass. Enjoy!

88. OATMEAL COOKIE SMOOTHIE

Total Time: 5 Minutes | Serving: 1

Ingredients

- 1 tbsp Nut Butter of Choice
- 1 cup of Milk of Choice
- 1/2 tsp Cinnamon
- 1 tbsp Maple Syrup
- 2 tbsp Rolled Oats
- Ice Cubes (to float on top)

Instructions

1. Put everything into your BlendJet and set it to two cycles.
2. Add more oats on top if you want to.
3. Put nut butter on top and enjoy!

89. CANDY CANE SMOOTHIE

Total Time: 5 Minutes | Serving: 1

Ingredients

- 1 tbsp Maple Syrup
- 1 cup of Milk of Choice
- 1/2 Frozen Banana
- 1/4 tsp Peppermint Extract
- 1/2 tsp Vanilla Extract
- 1/4 tsp Beet Powder (for color)
- Ice Cubes (to float on top)

Instructions

1. Combine all the ingredients in your BlendJet and blend for one to two cycles.
2. Cover the BlendJet with crushed candy canes and put a whole one on top to finish.

90. SNOWMAN SMOOTHIE

Total Time: 5 Minutes | Serving: 1

Ingredients

- 1/3 cup of Yogurt of Choice
- 1 tbsp Maple Syrup
- 1/2 tsp Vanilla Extract
- 1 cup of Milk of Choice
- 1/4 cup of Marshmallows
- 1/4 Banana

Instructions

1. Put everything in the BlendJet except the toppings. Blend for two to three cycles.
2. Add marshmallow fluff, marshmallows, and cinnamon on top. Have fun!

91. POST WORKOUT SMOOTHIE

Total Time: 5 Minutes | Serving: 1

Ingredients

- 1/3 cup of Almond Milk
- 1 Frozen Banana
- 1 tbsp Peanut Butter
- 2 tbsp Almond Yogurt
- Handful of Spinach

Instructions

1. Put 1/3 cup of almond milk, 2 tbsp almond yogurt, 1 tbsp peanut butter.
2. Put the lid back on your BlendJet and blend!
3. Add a handful of chopped spinach (minimal stems are recommended).
4. Put in one frozen banana.
5. Put the lid back on your BlendJet and blend until the mixture is smooth.

92. DETOX POWER SMOOTHIE

Total Time: 5 Minutes | Serving: 1

Ingredients

- 1 tbsp Peanut Butter
- 1 handful Spinach
- 1 Banana
- 1 tsp Chia Seeds
- 1/4 cup of Frozen Mixed Berries
- 1/3 cup of Milk of Choice

Instructions

1. Pour 1/3 cup of milk and 1 tbsp peanut butter.
2. Put the lid on your BlendJet and blend!
3. Add a handful of chopped spinach (minimal stems are recommended).
4. Put the lid on your BlendJet and blend!
5. Put in one banana.
6. Put the lid on your BlendJet and blend!
7. Put in 1/4 cup of mixed berries and 1 tsp of chia seeds.
8. Put the lid on your portable BlendJet blender and blend your healthy smoothie recipe until it is smooth.

93. PRE-WORKOUT SMOOTHIE

Total Time: 5 Minutes | Serving: 1

Ingredients

- 3/4 cup of Plant-Based Milk
- 1/4 cup of Frozen Banana
- 1/4 cup of Frozen Blueberries
- 1/4 cup of Oats
- 1/4 tsp Cinnamon

Instructions

1. Mix everything in your BlendJet for two to three cycles or until smooth.

94. DETOX SMOOTHIE

Total Time: 5 Minutes | Serving: 1

Ingredients

- 1 tbsp Lemon Juice
- 1 cup of Coconut Water
- 1/2 cup of Frozen Strawberries
- 1 pinch Cayenne Pepper
- 1/2 cup of Frozen Mango

Instructions

1. Put everything into your BlendJet and blend for one to two cycles.
2. Have fun!

95. WORKOUT SMOOTHIE

Total Time: 5 Minutes | Serving: 1

Ingredients

- 1/4 cup of Mango
- 1 Tropical Blue JetPack
- 1/4 cup of Banana
- 3/4 cup of Coconut Water

Instructions

1. Put everything into your BlendJet and blend for two cycles.
2. Sip and enjoy!

96. PREBIOTIC PROBIOTIC SMOOTHIE

Total Time: 5 Minutes | Serving: 1

Ingredients

- 1 tbsp Hemp Seeds
- 3/4 cup of Coconut Kefir
- 1/4 cup of Frozen Strawberries
- 1/4 cup of Frozen Mango
- 1 tbsp Agave

Instructions

1. Put everything into the BlendJet and let it run for one cycle. Have fun!

97. GREEN SMOOTHIE

Total Time: 5 Minutes | Serving: 1

Ingredients

- 1/2 cup of Mango
- 1/4 cup of Kale
- 1/2 Lime Juice
- 1 tbsp Maple Syrup
- 1/4 cup of Spinach
- 1/2 Banana
- 1 cup of Milk of Choice

Instructions

1. Put all your green smoothie recipe ingredients into the portable portable blender.
2. Blend for two to four times.
3. Sip and enjoy!

98. TROPICAL SMOOTHIE

Total Time: 5 Minutes | Serving: 1

Ingredients

- 1 cup of Coconut Water
- 1/2 cup of Frozen Pineapple
- 1/2 cup of Frozen Mango
- 1/4 cup of Coconut Yogurt

Instructions

1. Put all ingredients in your BlendJet and run it for one or two cycles.
2. Sip and enjoy!

99. ORANGE SMOOTHIE

Total Time: 5 Minutes | Serving: 1

Ingredients

- 1/2 cup of Carrots
- 2 Oranges
- 1 tsp Turmeric
- 1/2 cup of Frozen Banana
- 1 piece Ginger
- 1 1/2 cups of Water
- 1 cup of Ice Cubes

Instructions

1. Combine all the ingredients in your BlendJet. Run it for one cycle, and then enjoy!

100. IMMUNITY-BOOSTING SMOOTHIE

Total Time: 5 Minutes | Serving: 1

Ingredients

- 1/4 tsp Turmeric
- 2 tsp Chia Seeds
- 1/2 tsp Ginger
- 1/4 cup of Frozen Mango
- 3/4 cup of Orange Juice
- 1/2 tsp Cinnamon
- 1/2 Frozen Banana

Instructions

1. Put everything into your BlendJet and blend for two cycles.
2. Have fun!

Made in the USA
Columbia, SC
27 June 2025